COINS AND MONEY

# QUARTERS!

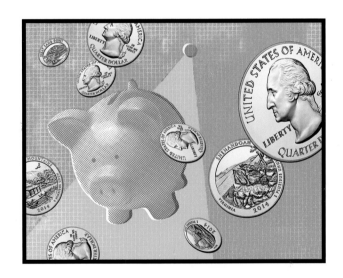

## LEE FITZGERALD

**PowerKiDS**
press™

New York

Published in 2016 by The Rosen Publishing Group, Inc.
29 East 21st Street, New York, NY 10010

First Edition

Editor: Katie Kawa
Book Design: Katelyn Heinle

Photo Credits: Cover, p. 1 (piggy bank) Lizzie Roberts/Ikon Images/Getty Images; cover, pp. 1, 5, 6, 9, 10, 13, 17, 22 (coins) Courtesy of U.S. Mint; cover, pp. 5, 6, 9, 10, 13, 14, 17, 18, 21, 24 (background design element) Paisit Teeraphatsakool/Shutterstock.com; pp. 5, 6, 9, 10 (vector bubbles) Dragan85/Shutterstock.com; pp. 10, 14, 24 (dollar bill) Fablok/Shutterstock.com; p. 13 (George Washington) JOE CICAK/E+/Getty Images; pp. 14, 17, 21 (vector bubble) LAN02/Shutterstock.com; p. 18 (vector bubble) gst/Shutterstock.com; pp. 18, 24 (quarter with eagle) rsooll/Shutterstock.com; p. 21 (New York quarter), (Texas quarter), (Arizona quarter) Tom Grundy/Shutterstock.com; p. 21 (Idaho quarter), (Washington quarter) mattesimages/Shutterstock.com; p. 22 (boy) ©iStockphoto.com/ChristopherBernard.

Library of Congress Cataloging-in-Publication Data

Fitzgerald, Lee.
Quarters! / by Lee Fitzgerald.
p. cm. — (Coins and money)
Includes index.
ISBN 978-1-4994-0723-5 (pbk.)
ISBN 978-1-4994-0722-8 (6 pack)
ISBN 978-1-4994-0503-3 (library binding)
1. Quarter-dollar — Juvenile literature. 2. Coins, American — Juvenile literature. I. Fitzgerald, Lee. II. Title.
CJ1835.F58 2016
737.4973—d23

Manufactured in the United States of America

CPSIA Compliance Information: Batch #WS15PK: For Further Information contact Rosen Publishing, New York, New York at 1-800-237-9932

# CONTENTS

A quarter is one kind of coin.
Coins are pieces of metal
used as money.

# DIME PENNY NICKEL

# QUARTER HALF-DOLLAR

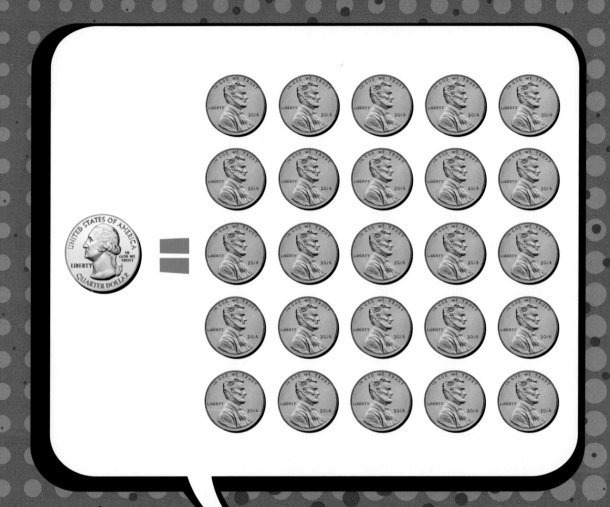

6

One quarter is worth 25 cents.
It is the same as 25 pennies.

One quarter is also the same as five nickels. One nickel is five cents.

9

A quarter is also known as a quarter dollar. One **dollar** is the same as four quarters.

George Washington is on the front of the quarter. He was the first president of the United States.

Washington is also on
the front of the dollar bill.

There are many different pictures on the backs of quarters.

Some quarters have a **bald eagle** on the back. This bird stands for the United States.

Each state has its own quarter.

David has 75 cents.
How many quarters is that?

# WORDS TO KNOW

bald eagle

dollar

# INDEX

# WEBSITES

Due to the changing nature of Internet links, PowerKids Press has developed an online list of websites related to the subject of this book. This site is updated regularly. Please use this link to access the list: www.powerkidslinks.com/cam/quar